By Air, Sea, and Land
Boats

Paul Stickland

WATERBIRD BOOKS
Columbus, Ohio

Ferry

Ferries carry passengers, vehicles, and cargo across bodies of water.

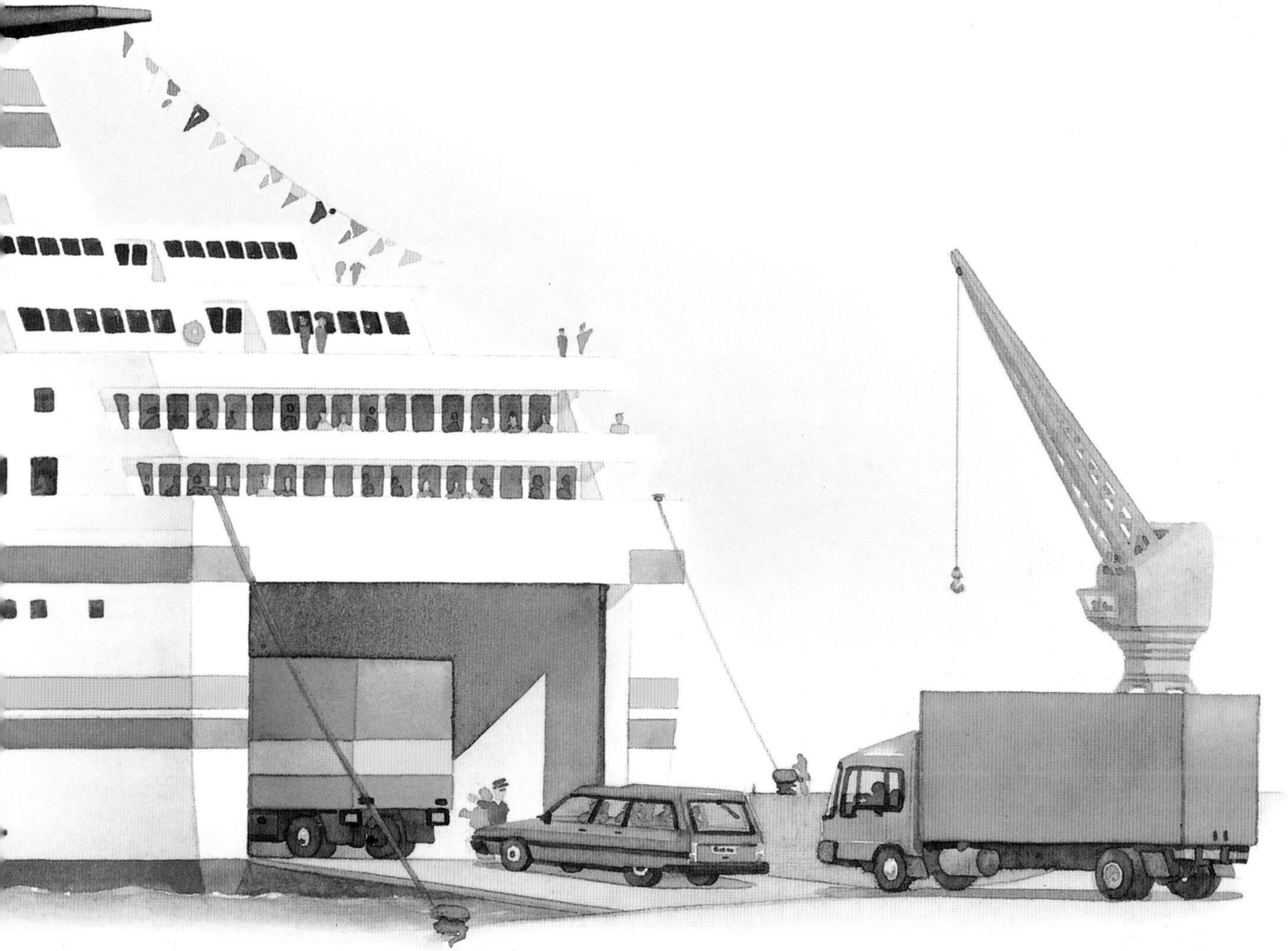

More About Ferries

Ferries carry people and their vehicles across the water.
Some ferries have restaurants and shops on the upper
decks where the passengers can spend their time during
the trip.

The ferry is controlled from the bridge, the raised platform at the front of the ship. From the bridge, the captain is able to see well enough to safely steer the ship in and out of the harbor.

Sailboat

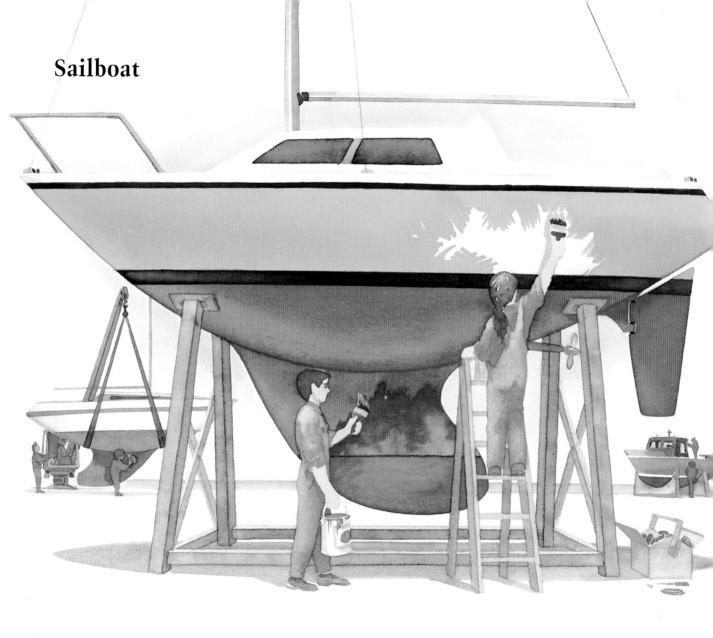

Sailboats have cloth sails that use the wind to push the sailboat through the water.

Rowboat

A **rowboat** is moved through the water with oars.

More About Sailboats

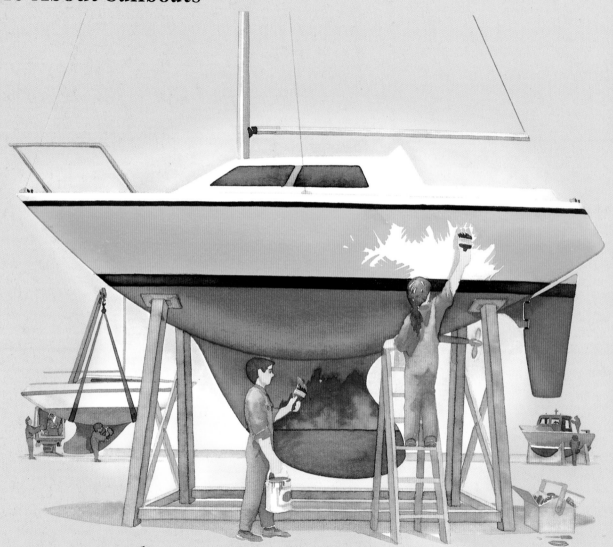

Sailboats are wind-powered boats that are used for fun and for racing. The lower part of a sailboat is called the *hull*. Sometimes, the hull needs to be repaired or repainted.

More About Rowboats

Rowboats are pulled through the water by oars.
The oars are held in place by oarlocks. A person
uses the oars to push the water back and the
rowboat forward.

Motorboat

Motorboats use large engines to travel very quickly through the water.

Hydrofoil

Hydrofoils are a high-speed boats.

More About Motorboats

Most motorboats are used for activities like waterskiing or fishing. Some motorboats have bedrooms, kitchens, and bathrooms below the main deck.

More About Hydrofoils

Hydrofoils have large metal plates, called *foils*, attached to the bottom of the boat. When the hydrofoil moves quickly, the foils lift the front of the boat out of the water.

Wooden Sailing Ship

Old **wooden sailing ships** have many sails that catch the wind and push the boat through the water quickly.

Ocean Liner

Ocean liners transport passengers and cargo across large bodies of water.

More About Wooden Sailing Ships

Even though most ships now use engines and are made out of metal, some still use sails and are made out of wood. These wooden ships require a large crew of sailors to make sure that everything is running smoothly.

More About Ocean Liners

Some ocean liners are used as cruise ships, taking people to different places for vacation. Ocean liners are so big that they need a powerful tugboat to help steer them safely into the harbor.

An **oil tanker** is a special ship that carries oil. Most of the ship is used to transport the oil from place to place.

More About Oil Tankers

The prow is the pointed front part of a ship. The shape of the prow helps the ship cut through the water and steady itself in rough seas.

Oil tankers are very slow, yet they are so big that they are hard to stop. Some oil tankers are almost a mile long. The oil that oil tankers transport comes from all over the world. It is used to make gasoline used for cars and boats.

What Did You Learn?

What are oars and paddles used for

How does this boat float?

What safety equipment is missing?

What is this boat called?

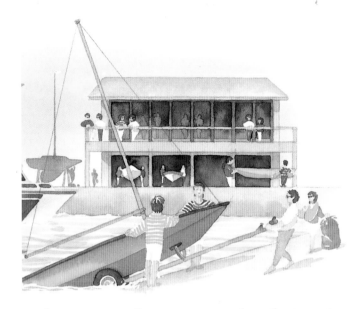

What does a tugboat do?

What are these people doing?

How do these sailboats move through the water?

This boat is full of air. This makes it light enough to float.

This boat is a luxury yacht. It is used for leisure.

Oars and paddles help steer and move boats through the water.

A tugboat helps pull a large tanker into the harbor.

The boy is not wearing a life jacket.

These people are loading their sailboat onto a trailer. This makes it easier to take the boat out of the water.

School Specialty
Children's Publishing

Copyright © Paul Stickland 1992, 2004
Designed by Douglas Martin.

This edition published in the United States of America in 2004
by Waterbird Books,
an imprint of School Specialty Children's Publishing,
a member of the School Specialty Family.
8720 Orion Place, Columbus, OH 43240-2111
www.ChildrensSpecialty.com

Library of Congress Cataloging-in-Publication is on file with the publisher.

ISBN 0-7696-3372-2
Printed in China.
1 2 3 4 5 6 7 8 MP 08 07 06 05 04

The wind in the sails of these boats pushes them through the water.